A DK PUBLISHING BOOK

Text Terry Martin
Project Editor Mary Atkinson
US Editor Camela Decaire
Senior Art Editor Jane Horne
Deputy Managing Editor Mary Ling
Production Louise Barratt
Consultant Theresa Greenaway
Picture Researcher Lorna Ainger

Additional photography by Peter Anderson, Jane Burton, Peter Chadwick, Geoff Dann, Mike Dunning, Steve Gorton, Frank Greenaway, Dave King, Tracy Morgan, Stephen Oliver, Stephen Shott, Kim Taylor, Matthew Ward, Jerry Young

First American Edition, 1996
2 4 6 8 10 9 7 5 3

Published in the United States by
DK Publishing, Inc.,
95 Madison Avenue,
New York, New York 10016
Copyright © 1996 Dorling Kindersley Limited, London

http://www.dk.com

Photographs copyright © 1992 Jerry Young (Why do elephants . . . ? polar bear; Why do crabs . . . ? crab top left, copperbanded butterflyfish)

A CIP catalog record for this book is available from the Library of Congress.
ISBN: 0-7894-1120-2
Color reproduction by Chromagraphics, Singapore. Printed and bound in Italy by L.E.G.O.

The publisher would like to thank the following for their kind permission to reproduce their photographs: **Bruce Coleman**: Jane Burton (Why don't cats hurt themselves . . . ?)c, (Why do snails carry . . . ?)c, Adrian Davies (Why can't I eat toadstools?)br, Francisco J. Erize (Why do crabs walk sideways?)c, Jeff Foott Productions (Why do crabs walk sideways?)bl, Hwange N. P. back cover c, (Why do elephants have long trunks?)c, Harald Lange (Why can't I eat toadstools?)c, Hans Reinhard front cover c, (Why do trees have leaves?)c, (Why do sunflowers . . . ?)c, Kim Taylor (Why do birds have feathers?)c; **The Image Bank**: John W. Banagan Endpapers

Questions

Why do elephants have long trunks?

Why don't cats hurt themselves when they fall?

Why do birds have feathers?

Why do crabs walk sideways?

Why do snails carry shells on their backs?

Why do trees have leaves?

Why do sunflowers turn toward the sun?

Why can't I eat toadstools?

WHY

do sunflowers face the sun?

Questions children ask about nature

Why do elephants

An elephant's long nose does more than smell. It acts as a trumpet, a hose, a snorkel, a hand to pluck leaves, and an arm to reach up high or to lift heavy objects.

Why don't polar bears get cold?
In the harsh, icy Arctic, polar bears can hunt for hours in freezing cold water thanks to bulky layers of fat called blubber under their thick, oily fur coats.

have long trunks?

Why do giraffes have long necks?
The world's longest neck doesn't just give a
giraffe a great view, it also allows it to munch
tasty leaves high on the tops of tall trees.

Why don't cats hurt

Cats are very fast and flexible. If they fall, they quickly twist around to land on their feet. They also have special leg joints that absorb the shock of hitting the hard ground.

Why are rabbits' ears so big?
Rabbits' ears are shaped to amplify sound. They can move

themselves when they fall?

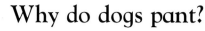

Why do dogs pant?
A dog pants and flops out its long, sloppy tongue to cool down. Water drying off its tongue cools a dog in the same way that sweat cools us.

their ears together or one at a time, too, to pick up the faintest noise of danger.

Feathers make good flight gear. They're not only warm, they're also lightweight, and have curved shapes that catch the wind, helping birds fly.

Why do roosters crow at dawn? The rooster gives an ear-splitting dawn performance to remind everyone that he's number one – the strongest male in the roost.

have feathers?

**Why do ducks
have webbed feet?**
Ducks have amazing "paddle
power." Their webbed feet
propel them speedily through
water like the oars on a boat.

Why do crabs walk

To avoid a messy tangle of eight long legs, crabs scuttle sideways – especially during fast getaways. One set of legs pulls and the other pushes. Then zoom, they're off!

Why do whales spurt water?
Whales take huge lungfuls of air before diving underwater. Unlike fish, they must come back up to

sideways?

Why don't fish drown?
Like us, fish need to
breathe oxygen. But while our lungs
are designed to take oxygen out of
the air, fishes' gills are able to
take oxygen out
of water.

take another breath. When they
exhale, warm, moist air snorts out
of their nostril, or blowhole, turning
into a fountain of water and air.

Why do snails carry

A snail's shell is like a camper van – it's a mobile home that it carries around. When it senses danger, it quickly curls up inside its shell.

Why don't flies fall when they walk upside down?
A fly's sharp claws are no use on a smooth upside-down surface like a ceiling. But it also has hairy pads on its feet that work like suction cups. Fancy footwork!

shells on their backs?

Why do ants travel in lines?
After discovering food, an ant rushes back to its nest, leaving a smelly trail behind it. Other ants then follow their noses to find the food.

Why don't worms have legs?
Earthworms live underground, creating deep tunnels as they wriggle about. Their long, thin, legless bodies have stiff bristles and strong muscles that are perfect for pushing through soil.

Why do trees

Like tiny solar panels, leaves soak up sunlight and convert its energy into the food a tree needs.

Why do pine trees have cones?
Pine trees take a long time to grow their soft, delicate seeds. The seeds grow inside cones, where they're protected from rain and hungry animals by the cone's woody scales.

have leaves?

Why does a tree stump have lots of rings?
Each year a spring growth spurt produces a ring inside a tree trunk. By counting all the rings, you can figure out a tree's age.

Why do sunflowers turn

Sunflowers' beautiful yellow heads and green leaves follow the sun across the sky, making warm landing pads for bees and catching lots of energy-giving light.

Why do plants have to be watered?
Next time it rains, think about the plants outside. They use rainwater to

toward the sun?

Why do cactuses have spines?
Cactuses are the roughest, toughest plants in the desert. Their sharp spines protect them from hungry animals and collect precious water from dewdrops.

make food and to hold up their leaves. Indoor plants would die if we didn't give their roots "rain."

Why can't I eat

Toadstools might look like edible mushrooms, but there are lots of different fungi, and many are highly poisonous.

Why do fungi grow on tree stumps?
Many fungi feed on rotting wood. As they eat, they grow deep into the wood, helping break it down.

toadstools?

Why do some fungi have frilly gills?
Gills are launching pads for millions of tiny seedlike spores, which may soon grow into new fungi.

Why does food get moldy?
A mold is a type of fungus. Its tiny spores float in the air like specks of dust. When a spore lands on food, it grows into another mold.